My Dating Life,
My Choice

by Molly Hillig Rodriguez, RN, BSN, MPH

and Ken Carlson, PCC

Published and Printed in the USA.

ISBN: 978-0-692-85396-2

Cover design by Jim Schwertfeger

Table of Contents

Chapter One

Two Approaches to Dating: A Female and Male Perspective

Chapter Two

Who Am I in High Heels? Uncovering the Authentic Self

Chapter Three

The Date Review: Don't Go It Alone

Chapter Four
Meeting the Friends: An Experience in Culture

Chapter Five
Meeting the Parents: The Family Dynamic

Chapter Six
Are We Serious? Breaking the Iceberg

Chapter Seven
The Bedroom: Talk About It

Chapter Eight

Can I Trust You? Being Your Full Self

Chapter Nine

The Crucible of Growth: Change

Coachable Moments

Foreward

My Dating Life, My Choice is a spectacular book about relationship issues and dating advice. It is ideal for dating enthusiasts of all skill-levels who want to discover the thrill of authentic romantic love, the type of love that makes you spread your wings and fly. If you, as so many have, experienced the opposite: relationships that demean or suffocate you, this book will help you find the "true love" that we are all striving to achieve and keep in our lives.

Its co-authors, Molly and Ken, do a wonderful job in showing readers how to accept and value themselves, practice self-love, and create authentic relationships. They reveal the foundation pieces of emotionally fulfilling relationships. The authors guide the readers through the process of getting out of the dark tunnel of delusions and heading into the light of authentic love by following the simple action steps discussed in each chapter.

My Dating Life sends you on an inward journey to help you overcome your fear of being alone and pushes you along so you can build a structure of self-care which is essential in achieving your goal of emotional fulfillment. It shows you how to turn your weaknesses into strengths, put your own needs first, and discover who you truly are. You will come to believe that high-quality relationships are possible, when you're willing to work for them. Truly the sky's the limit!

Violeta Kadieva, PhD,
LMFT-Associate, AAMFT Approved Supervisor
Assistant Professor of Graduate Counseling Program
Texas Wesleyan University

Introduction

This book is about helping you become a better dater. Through this book, you'll learn how to identify your love beliefs and patterns by examining your past experiences. You will become able to utilize what you learn about yourself to make small but consistent changes in your life and start having the kind of dating experience you want, one that is fulfilling and healthy. You'll begin to understand why you do what you do, your motives and intentions, and specifically who you are as a dater and who you want to become.

Storytelling is one of the ways humans transmit experience to one another. Therefore, in each chapter, you will read personal stories of dating successes and flops from both a female (Molly) and male (Ken) perspective. Molly and Ken's stories are illustrative of the journey of two people who were each at different points in their dating lives, who had arrived at their own personal intersection with a different set of behaviors and beliefs, yet they felt it imperative to improve the quality of their relationships. They reviewed and utilized their past as an asset rather than a liability.

Plus, you will receive input from a relationship coach. After each story, we will look at what was said by Molly and Ken through the lens of this coach, which serves to underscore the importance of having your own coach to guide you through this process.

At the end of each section there are five questions for further consideration, to act as homework, as you try practicing what you have learned in all your relationships.

This book will challenge you to take some steps, examine your past behavior, and shape a new and better dating self. We're positive that, if you take the material to heart and put it into practice, you will see different and satisfying results. But, in all likelihood, this book is only the beginning of your journey, as you will want to continue to grow throughout your life, with the help of a coach who will show you how these thoughts have helped them become a better dater.

About the Authors

Ken Carlson, PCC has over 15 years of experience as a corporate leader and over 10 years of experience as a coach and trainer. He is a certified professional coach and leader and has helped hundreds of unique clients from all over the world. Ken's roles have included an Implementation Director of a Fortune 300 organization, Instructor of Chemistry at a Chicago area university, Founder and Owner of a Leadership Training & Coaching organization Authentic Development. He understands the challenges of being on the fast track at work while also wanting to make a lasting impact in all areas of life.

Ken believes that relationships are the most important things in life, particularly those with his children being the most critical, their influence being the only thing that will outlive and outlast him. He loves to travel and is learning Spanish to broaden his cultural compassion. Ken loves the outdoors and relishes a canoe trip to the Boundary Waters Canoe Area as often as possible. He is also a triathlon freak, having done eight in the last 18 months—including an IronMan 70.3 in July 2010.

Molly Hillig Rodriguez, RN, BSN, MPH, Relationship Coach has developed and hosted seven international retreats structured around the empowerment of personal relationships. Her professional experience includes relationship coaching, Salsa dancing, nursing, and public health. Molly is bilingual and has traveled to 15 countries. She brings the best of her energy and expertise to every event and uses humor and movement to engage her audience, as she says "When I am not with my husband and son, I am hiking or dancing in my kitchen."

She loves life and feels most fulfilled when those around her are successful. Molly's personal dedication is to share her knowledge of relationships, dating, and living a radiant life in order to help her clients achieve their dreams of health and happiness. Her belief is "if we dedicate ourselves to a deeper yearning and are not afraid to make mistakes, then we create the relationships we want. When we have great relationships with ourselves, our home and work performance thrives, and as a result, our communities thrive. I understand the biology, physiology, and psychology behind strong and healthy relationships, it is more than just 'communication.' It starts with working on ourselves."

How to Use This Book

The best way to utilize this book is by being in relationships with other people — best friend, coach, therapist — and apply what you learn here to each and every interaction in your life.

The homework questions at the end of each chapter are essential steps in helping you retain and put into practice what you've learned. When it asks you to write, don't just think about the answers in your head, write them down. They will become more real for you.

This book will be helpful for anyone looking to improve their dating life, no matter where you feel you are along that path, a bare beginner or an experienced pro.

There are no guarantees in relationships. You may still get hurt, but part of love is learning to be with hurt and upset. If you accept the concepts outlined in this book you will grow from the experience and put it to good use in the future. There is nothing more enriching than a relationship built on authentic love.

Chapter 1

Two Approaches to Dating:
A Female and Male Perspective

Everyone begins their journey of improving their dating lives at a different place. And that's OK. The first step is to recognize where you are and how you currently approach dating. It's not about ignoring or forgetting your past, it's about embracing it and putting it to good use.

One Woman's Approach

"You yourself, as much as anybody in the entire universe, deserve your love and affection" —Buddha

What's wrong with him? I wondered, why isn't he responding to my texts?

"Sam" was attractive and seemed like he had his shit together. I liked the conversations we had, he seemed engaged, and he liked to travel, which was appealing to me. I felt like we were a great match — so why wasn't he calling? I played it cool, trying not to show my enthusiasm for our first "hangout

1

session." What Sam didn't know was that I was planning a second and third hangout session and even our marriage. Bottom line, I wanted Sam to show me that he felt the same way about me as I felt about him. Couldn't he see that?

Coachable Moment: A Date Vs. "Hanging Out"

There's a big difference between "going on a date" and "hanging out". Traditional courtship involves the man taking the woman someplace in public to get to know one another. The woman should be able to tell the difference between this and sitting on his couch watching movies. The man, however, may not consider them to be different things. If you want to be taken out on a date, you should make it clear that you don't consider "hanging out" to be a date. A date creates anticipation and an environment of love. A hangout session a simple cop-out to the real deal.

Despite his apparent lack of interest, I didn't want to lose Sam, so I wanted to make sure I didn't make any of the same mistakes I made in my past. I thought a lot about my past approach to dating, and I realized that I dated like a teenager. What I mean by that is I approached it from insecurity and inexperience. I wanted so desperately to be accepted and was too inexperienced to know how to and how *not* to date. I was unable to learn from my previous mistakes and was therefore doomed to repeat them. I wanted everyone to cherish and approve of me, even though I did not cherish or approve of myself. I lacked the personal wherewithal to understand and accept that this sort of trying to "fit a square peg into a round hole" approach didn't work, that it doesn't work when you're an adult, if it ever even worked as a teenager.

After a failed serious relationship, shortly before I met Sam, I was with a guy who watched movies end- lessly and slept in until 1 pm

> **"I wanted everyone to cher- ish and approve of me, even though I did not cherish or approve of myself."**

on the weekends. To me, Sam seemed like a gem compared to him. My previous relationship with the Afternoon Snoozer started the same way it had with Sam. We went on a few coffee dates; he also didn't respond to my texts but my persistence led to more dates. Eventually we hooked up and then I started planning our future in my mind. Romantic? I think not.

I thought Sam was different than the Afternoon Snoozer because he was a go-getter. That's why it baffled me when he didn't respond to my texts and rarely took me out on dates. Well, honestly he didn't even call them dates, just "hang out" sessions. When I wouldn't get a response from him I would think "doesn't he know what an awesome girl I am?" I was busy planning our next relationship move while he was plan- ning what he was going to eat for lunch.

"I'll Have The Usual."

Seeing the Pattern

"The most splendid achievement of all is the constant striving to surpass yourself and to be worthy of your own approval" —Denis Waitley

My experience with Sam didn't feel unfamiliar, with me usually waiting around to hear from guys after our "hangout sessions." I wanted to be sure there was a second date, as an attempt to satisfy my insatiable desire to feel loved and wanted. In hindsight, I was desperate, so I threw myself at non-winners (i.e. losers). I had been burned and was resentful. My experiences usually ended in disappointment and pain, even though in the beginning I was so darned optimistic. I felt quite hopeful initially, only to see everything turn sour, and I was unable to understand the reason for the pattern.

Coachable Moment: Winners Vs. Losers

I don't mean to suggest there are winner and loser human beings, everyone has value. When it comes to dating, however, there's no sense trying to find something in someone who is unwilling or unable to provide it. It's either there or it's not. Think of it as going into a hardware store to buy milk. It may be helpful, therefore, to categorize your dates as winners and losers. You wouldn't hang on to a losing lottery ticket, would you?

In my past, I dated without realizing or respecting my self-value. In fact, I didn't know what "self-value" even meant. I was desperate for affirmation from others, especially men. This led to a lot of short, shitty relationships which had the common theme of me falling for the losers and chasing the good ones away. I thought this was just what dating was. I couldn't understand why this seemed to be the pattern, but my behavior showed that in a way I was, in effect, getting as much respect from others as I was giving myself: little to none. My pain and frustration were trying to tell me some-

> **"I was desperate for affirmation from others, especially men."**

thing, but I wasn't listening, or at least I was unable to, until I had experienced enough suffering.

"What Changed?!"

Starting With Yourself

"Love yourself first and everything else falls into line." —Lucile Ball

Now I appreciate an important element that was missing in my dating life: self-love. I had clearly learned through my life experiences that I was not valuable and my behaviors illustrated that I felt like I did not deserve honorable, genuine and authentic love. So guess what? I didn't get it.

I see that a lot of women today date this way, repeating the same cycle. They create stories through texts, try to build a relationship through email, fantasize about their future with the person after the first date, or sleep with the guy too soon.

I'd even continue to date guys that I wasn't that interested in because I didn't want to be alone. I was just hoping to find someone great and pin them down so they would love me for the rest of my life. I thought all that was needed to accomplish this was the right technique, something like a magic trick!

I saw that my dating system was a fatal one and that no one ever won in this type of dynamic...especially me. So, it became clear that I had a choice to make and I made it! I decided to learn to love myself first, my whole self...even the parts of me that I despised.

This empowered choice came after I started looking at women and men in my life who seemed to be fulfilled in their relationships. They seemed to create love, not react to it. I noticed these special folks seemed to enjoy the whole process of dating — the good, the bad and the ugly. They saw love as an experience, something that caused them to learn and grow. They beamed with self-love, self-value and authenticity. This self-love concept was new to me and a little scary. However, I wanted in!

So, I dumped Sam.

I decided to explore my internal pain, which was responsible for dimming my self-love. Then, I started to fall in love with myself. I let go of control; I enjoyed the ride of dating. I finally started to see that dating is not about control, sleeping around, or settling down, but is about learning and growing myself and my heart.

> **"I decided to learn to love myself first, my whole self... even the parts of me that I despised."**

What I continue to learn about myself and my relationships is that love can be a growthful experience that brings fun, joy and richness or it can be a cycle that seems to end with the same negative outcome. I ultimately get to decide. To make dating a powerful movement of love in my life, I must first love myself. This is my new approach to relationships. I find it has helped with all my relationships: finances, body, friends, family and God. It is not an easy journey or an overnight transformation, but I stick with the process. It is rewarding.

One Man's Approach

"The last time I dated was before the internet."

When my marriage ended and I found myself single — truly single — for the first time since I was a Senior in high school. I felt lost and was filled with questions. What type of person did I want to be with? Did I even want a relationship right now? What had changed in the last 20 years?

A lot had changed, apparently. Technology had changed the way people interact and I was completely ignorant about online dating. When I was a teenager, I met girls at Wendy's where I worked or at school. There was a constant source of girls that I could crush on and attempt to date. Now, as a 40-year-old in the suburbs, I felt like my options were limited. I wasn't meeting women anywhere — at least women that I wanted to be with. I was at a loss as to where to start this dating journey, and although I didn't have much hope, I certainly wasn't going to just sit on the sidelines.

Honestly, it had been just a few months since the end of my marriage and I was still processing all that had gone wrong. As some sort of self-torture, I went to a Def Leppard concert with my sister and hated almost every song in their catalog. *Love Hurts! Pour Some Sugar On Me,* etc. At the intermission, I was still left sitting with all that had happened and I wanted desperately to make some sense out of my thoughts, with the hope of discovering what I really wanted. In that moment, I typed an email into my Blackberry with a list of what I felt I deserved. It was a way for me to take a stand and make a commitment to myself that I wanted my future to be different.

I knew I wanted to live authentically, so a good deal of the traits that I wanted in a relationship partner coincided with my own desires for myself. Speaking of authenticity — the truth is, no one does any of these things perfectly, so the idea wasn't to find the perfect person — the idea was to get clear about what was important to me as I reentered the world of women.

> **"...although I didn't have much hope, I certainly wasn't going to just sit on the sidelines."**

Here is what I wrote in my Blackberry:

What I want:

- A woman that is crazy about me
- A woman that will tell me the truth even if I don't want to hear it
- A woman that knows that I am imperfect and will make big and small mistakes
- A smart, independent woman
- Someone that lives on a journey of growth
- A best friend that I can partner with in life

Then, I just went out. I have a buddy that's always up for a trip to a bar or park or whatever, so two or three nights a week we went out. My goal each time was to just have a great conversation with a woman. So I did — and have had some amazing conversations with all types of women.

"What's *Different* About Me?"

Standing Out In A Crowd

"If you're 100% yourself, then you're going to be different no matter what. I have this self-honesty approach as opposed to an ego that a lot of musicians put up. I can be myself, and that's just enough to stand out." —Shamir

My main strategy about having great conversations is to just stay curious and remain brutally honest about myself and what I want. I only really want to hang out with people that like the real me anyway. I don't mind being vulnerable and I think vulnerability is an absolute requirement for meaningful talks. I've found that women are VERY attracted to the REALness that comes with being open about both the good and the bad. I think both men and women need to acknowledge that we are all imperfect so they're given permission to be less than perfect as well. People who aren't about being real are not right for you anyway, so why waste time and energy on them?

On one occasion, my buddy and I went to New York City for the weekend. The best day of the trip was literally one of the most fun days of my life. It was a Saturday. We started out with some breakfast at Balthazar's in Soho and then a trip to Central Park for a 10k run. My "great conversation" intention was in full-swing and we ended up meeting two women WHILE we were running. I even exchanged numbers with one of them as she was considering hiring me by the end of the conversation. After our run, we sat down in Times Square to eat our lunch on a curb next to two beautiful women. It turns out they were single and soon I was lost in a great conversation with a woman. I was in awe of how the universe had provided, allowing me to engage in such a rich conversation 1,000 miles from home. We invited them out to dinner and had a wonderful evening together.

I keep having great conversations when I go out and these conversations have turned into some wonderful dates.

Being in my 40's and single is an adventure all its own. I won't pretend that it's always easy and I've heard the naysayers tell me that it is much easier for guys than girls. But I think it is really just as hard as we make it. I decided to have fun with my life — however it looked. Decide to have fun with your life and I think you will discover even more abundance will come your way, as it did in my own life.

As one of my friends said just this week, "After five years of trying to find a guy to make me happy, the moment I decided to just make myself happy, I met someone special."

Through the lens of a Relationship Coach
Molly Hillig Rodriguez, RN, BSN, MPH

It may be hard to believe, but the woman in the first story used to be me. Looking at the woman's perspective now through the lens of a relationship coach, it is clear that there comes a moment in our dating lives when we have to grow up. We realize the way we have been approaching dating and love is all wrong. It's not about trying hard, it's about growth and learning to love yourself. The more we love ourselves the more love we have to give. People who fight so hard to succeed in a relationship without understanding why they really want it often end up rendering the opposite of their intended result. Instead of harmony and love they create discord and misery.

It's common to want to "jump ahead" in relationships when you meet someone you really like. If you meet them and there is this "spark" you want to make sure that you do everything you can to kindle it. So you start planning for the future instead of just enjoying the moment. We're afraid, perhaps, that if it doesn't work out we will be failures, we will be alone, would have wasted our time, or whatever we are afraid of. Yes, we have to recognize our fears and admit them to ourselves and others.

Molly was not dating to learn more about herself or discover love, she was fighting to not be alone. When people feel desperately alone they will do anything to try to assuage that feeling, even disregard their own values. She didn't see that her love story needed to start with personal enrichment. This is an inward journey where humans learn how to understand what their beliefs are, both about themselves and others, as well as their behaviors toward themselves and others, and how they connect with the rest of humanity and the universe (or, if you prefer, God).

Some folks read books, journal, hire coaches, attend church or seminars for enrichment. They challenge themselves to become a better person for themselves, friends, familyships and the world around them. When you are ready to look at your beliefs, behaviors, and how you play a role in humanity, your self-love, self-value and authenticity grow!

A journey of personal enrichment is not easy but it is honorable. Perhaps you are already on it. You are, after all, reading this book, and you want to discover how to become a better dater. So congratulations are in order! You've shown the willingness to open yourself up to the possibility that it can and will happen in your life as it did in mine.

What Ken is saying here is that he decided to put his needs first. He wanted to experience dating through authenticity. He wanted to be loved for who he is and what he believes he deserves. Ken was willing to make a claim in his life and he gave himself homework to practice — having great conversations with women. In these conversations, he creates abundance in his life. This is a powerful choice — imagine having the power in your own life to create fulfilling, worthwhile interactions. You have this power! Ken admits he does not have it all figured out but he has made an adventure out of dating.

Ken took the pain he was suffering through and turned

it into positive action. He wrote down what he wanted, even though it was undoubtedly difficult. Many people never inventory or make a list of what they want and are all the more frustrated when they don't feel like they're getting what they want or need. How can you know what you're looking for in a relationship unless you make it clear? Honesty with self is difficult. A lot of times we would rather deceive ourselves in order to avoid looking at painful aspects of our lives. But nothing is more rewarding than self-examination.

> **"When you are ready to look at your beliefs, behaviors, and how you play a role in humanity, your self-love, self-value and authenticity grow!"**

Moreover, Ken decided to be himself, rather than put on an act that he thought would be pleasing to others, an act that would ultimately turn against him as perhaps it did in his previous two marriages. Shakespeare wrote "To Thine Own Self Be True" and to paraphrase, when you are true to yourself you can't be false with others. That is to say, keep the focus on you and the rest will follow.

Acceptance of one's self, every single tiny part of it, is necessary for self-awareness, self-care, self-value and self-love. We have to realize our strengths and our weaknesses, endeavor to improve where we can, but ultimately accept our imperfections and learn from our mistakes, which arise out of our humanness. To sum it up in a word: authenticity. Authentic people know who they are and accept others for who they are as well.

5 Action Steps To Practice As Homework:

1. Ask yourself and journal about "What is your intention behind dating?" This powerful question can help you understand who you are attracting.

2. Map your relationship past on a poster board. Write down each relationship, noting how you approached it. What were the highlights?, How did it end? What did you learn about yourself?

3. Start looking for a good coach. Look for someone that is well-trained and works well with you.

4. Write down what you want in a dating partner. What do you discover by doing so? Is it difficult to put down your wants in writing? Do you feel like you shouldn't ask for a lot? What does that say about your ideas about dating? Are you afraid?

5. Look at your family's and friends' approaches to dating. Find people whose approach you respect and ask them how they did it.

Chapter 2:

Who Am I in High Heels?
Uncovering the Authentic Self

Who are you, or who do you *appear to be,* at least from a dating perspective? If you're honest with yourself, you may find that this outward persona you portray when you're on a date isn't who you really are. You may discover that it's actually part of the problem. Why wear a mask when your real face is what people love?

Molly's Story

"You put high heels on and you change." —Manolo Blahnik

I had three big heartbreak relationships in my past that usually ended in cheating. I was often the cheater. When I reflect on these relationships, it is easy to see who I was in high heels or how I showed up in dating: I represented a false version of myself to men — that I was a woman who was laid back, loving and warm. Or at least it looked like I was trying. The truth was, I believed all men were assholes — and the only way to get my needs met was through control and manipulation.

I would plan my dates, from beginning to end. This was the only way to ensure my needs were met, my strongest need at that time being certainty. I knew the "just right" dress to wear and only applied my makeup lightly. Men swooned. I was highly agreeable, laughed at jokes I hated, and shared stories of my world travels. The men I attracted liked my "go with the flow" front, but that's all it was. During the date, I would try and guess what he was thinking and respond accordingly. It was hard to stay with my own thoughts and feelings. At the end of the night I always insisted on paying half. Nights usually ended in the bedroom, and it was unfulfilling. Then I would get bored and move on to the next guy, thinking it would be different.

"Can I Trust You?"

Do Something Differently

"The Definition of Insanity is doing the same thing over and over, expecting different results." —Albert Einstein.

A close friend of mine mentioned to me that I needed to start trusting people more. Her comment knocked me on my ass. That was the first time I was able see that I did not trust men...but even deeper than that, I did not trust myself (I am, after all, a person too). I got a glimpse at the self-fulfilling prophecy I created in my life: men are assholes so I act in such a way to make that appear true. Sure, I've met some assholes, but generalizing to the point where I think *all* men are assholes, that's just a way of avoiding seeing people as individuals, as people, people who have a varying degree of strengths and weaknesses. A way I knew I could change this self-fulfilling prophecy was to begin with changing me and discovering where this belief came from.

Coachable Moment: Looking the Part

It occurs to me that women are well-practiced at how to present themselves in the most pleasing light to the men in their lives. In fact, from the moment they hit puberty, they are under the scrutiny of society to be poised, seductive, thin and not too powerful. Unfortunately, this often leaves the female with a false sense of self, one that was engineered to please, and not be authentic. Perhaps males also learn that their desires are designed to be catered to in this fashion, which creates a seemingly-lopsided dynamic, and anything that falls short of this makes it appear like the woman is being disagreeable and/or the man is an asshole!

I hired a great coach for guidance and I started becoming more authentic. I looked at the boundaries that were absent in my life. I cut ties with my so-called "friends with benefits." I committed to not going home with guys on the 1st, 2nd or 3rd date.

Perhaps, the most painful and purposeful exploration was that of my absent father and the void I was trying to fill. I wanted love, real love. For the first time, I set personal boundaries for relationships with men. I would remind myself that men are not assholes. When I would catch myself engaging in behaviors that allowed men to mistreat me, I would pause and reflect. I stopped laughing at jokes just to make them feel OK and I loosened my grip of control. I thought more deeply about the woman I wanted to become. Holding onto that vision guided me into making better decisions.

I was surprised at how quickly I started attracting higher -quality men.

So, when Chris walked up to me as I was strolling down Michigan Avenue in Chicago, I wasn't surprised. He was confident and wouldn't let me take the reins in every situation. He was high quality. Chris (my now husband) and I started our relationship with truth and genuine laughter. On our first date, I shared about how I had made mistakes in my last relationships and that I wanted things to be different. He shared about things in life that really scared him. I laughed for real at his jokes that I found funny and frowned when I did not.

> **"For the first time, I set boundaries for relationships with men."**

"How am I showing up?" is an important question I ask myself on a daily basis. It gives me time to reflect on me and my actions. I am still learning that I am responsible for the way I represent myself to the world and the beliefs I hold. I if I had not been willing to look at myself and change, I would still be cheating and trying to control dating. Worst of all, I would have never created love.

Ken's Story

"For the apparel oft proclaims the man." —Shakespeare

Well, I don't wear high heels...but I do wear a nice shirt and I've got some stylish shoes that I only bring out when I want to stand out and look good. But the question here isn't what I wear — it's who I really am on those first few dates.

First, a story; it was a beautiful summer evening and I had chosen a Tapas restaurant for our first date. My date and I quickly fell into a wonderful conversation about life and what we each wanted in a romantic relationship. She confided in me that she was looking for the fairy tale — she was still hopeful that it existed out there. I so agreed with her — I wanted the fairy tale too — but with two divorces in my past, an idealized version of a relationship seemed a little hard to believe in. Then I remembered my favorite fairy tale and said to her, "I don't know if we can have the typical fairy tale, but Shrek was a fairy tale and I know that the soundtrack was amazing and they had a ton of fun." We laughed heartily and moving forward Shrek became a theme of our relationship as we became more and more involved with each other.

> **"...the question here isn't what I wear — it's who I really am on those first few dates."**

Why did I choose to be fully me? Why bother being authentic? To have my outsides match my insides.

"Stick With What You Know."

The Importance of Being Yourself

"If there's any definition to being perfect,
you're perfect at being yourself." —Zendaya

I showed up as me. Of course, I wanted to impress her and yet I knew that if she didn't know the real me — the one with all the baggage — it wasn't going to work out in the end. Authenticity is a theme for me in my life and I do my best to take that into my dating life as well.

"The truth will set you free, but first it will piss you off."
—Gloria Steinem et al

Just recently, I was having one of these first date conversations and I was talking about how much fun I was having fun in the dating scene recently. I could tell by the look my date gave me and the tone of her voice that she was aghast. She asked me why I would tell her about other women I was dating. I was a little surprised because we had just met online a couple of days prior. Her perspective was that once you choose someone to pursue, you should only pursue them. I appreciated her perspective, but I didn't agree with it. As our conversation continued, she expressed appreciation for my honesty. The truth was that she wanted an honest man even more than she wanted a man who would tell her she was the only woman in the world and be dishonest by doing so. She had to decide, on the spot, what was more important: hearing the truth, or some lie she wanted to believe more. I didn't know if our relationship would progress from there, but at least we both agreed that honesty is critical.

Coachable Moment: The Hard Truth About Honesty

It is remarkable how much we, as humans, do not tell the truth. Even those of us who feel we are honest and are righteous about our truthfulness are often guilty of spreading little white lies. Dishonesty has many forms:

- Telling a lie
- Withholding the truth
- Saying one thing and doing another
- Sharing half of the truth
- Not speaking from the heart
- Agreeing with something that you actually do not agree with
- Not speaking up
- Avoiding what is really there

It is a hard to give and receive feedback honestly. That is why we often withhold the truth for fear of the damage it might do, hurting someone's feelings and/or being viewed as mean. So, we often tell people what we think they want to hear. It's a vicious circle of disintegrity that can leave everyone confused about how to act in certain situations. The truth hurts sometimes and when we have learned to love like a grow-up, it is essential.

"Say what you mean, mean what you say,
but don't say it mean." —Unknown

Coachable Moment: Responsible Honesty

That doesn't give me carte blanche to say whatever I want to say though. Keep it in the bounds of good taste. Show respect. Some people brag about how they're "brutally honest" with no filter between their mouth and their brain. That simply doesn't work. Manners and grace, when practiced often, become part of your authentic self and make you more available and loving to others, whether it's with the auto mechanic or your date.

Through the lens of a Relationship Coach
Molly Hillig Rodriguez, RN, BSN, MPH

What I find striking about Ken's experience is his willingness to look at his past failed relationships and learn from them. He sees the value of accurately sharing his feelings, thoughts, and behaviors honestly; Ken wants authenticity in his life. He is practicing this fiercely in his dating career and seeing different results.

Molly is saying that how she sees herself changes everything. When she was solely confident in her outward appearance, that's all that the men in her life got from her — the superficial Molly. However, when she sees her full self, both her amazingness and flaws, and brings that to the world, she can bring all of who she is to the men in her life, and the result of is a more authentic and ultimately fulfilling relationship.

What others think of you is none of your business" —Unknown

It's easy to lose focus and become more concerned with what you think other people are thinking rather than paying attention only to your own thoughts and feelings. It takes a conscious presence to keep the focus on you and how you are showing up, but when you do, the rest will follow as it should. As humans, we are mentally hardwired to care what others think and their judgements of us. That is why "we put on our high heels" for first dates. Even folks who say they do not care what others think are probably lying. We all seek acceptance on some level from our peers, but what is important here is that *you* accept who *you* are. The more you accept who you are, the more others will fall in love with you the real you.

As a coach, I often recommend my clients to try "wearing" one of their values when they enter a situation. Here's what I mean: think about what matters most to you and write a list of the values you hold most dear. Honesty, integrity, kindness, friendship, humor, playfulness, and sassiness are just a few characteristics that you might value. Once you've made that list, pick one that you want to try on as you enter a given situation. Put it on like a coat — fully embody it — and just remind yourself constantly that you are going to hold onto this value during the conversation *no matter what.*

I believe each of us are magnificently unique. When we show the truest version of ourselves, I believe that there is a level of attractiveness that is undeniable.

Who you show up as during those first dates can make all the difference in the world. Good luck!

---

5 Action Steps To Practice As Homework:

1. Hire a damn good coach, someone who can stand to be with you and all of your shit. Explore, as I explored, the things you like and hate about yourself. I haven't figured it all out, but as a result, I'm on the path of self-love.

2. Set an intention before each date to be your real self.

3. Notice when you are exaggerating, avoiding, or obliging.

4. Journal about your past relationships, writing about what you liked and disliked about each one. What are the commonalities in each category? Are you seeing a pattern?

5. Reflect on what self-fulfilling prophecies you may have. Do they usually seem to come true? Why is that? Does it show you, if nothing else, that you have the power to make choices and affect your dating life for the better?

Chapter 3

The Date Review:
Don't Go It Alone

Don't let your own thoughts and feelings be the sole perspective when reviewing a date. It's important to have a friend's perspective, which is bound to be more objective than your own. In the very least it's wise to have as much information as you can before making a decision. Think of it as the buddy system — and that your old habitual dating brain is like a bad neighborhood. Don't go there alone!

Molly's Story

"The real man smiles in trouble, gathers strength from distress, and grows brave by reflection." —Thomas Paine

When I met my future husband Chris, I knew there was something different about him, or more accurately, something different about me. I had evolved in my dating. Through this evolutionary process, I had attracted a different kind of man than I was used to.

Prior to Chris, after each date I spent hours in the anxious zone, analyzing how the date went. I asked myself questions like "Did he like me?" "What did I dislike about him?" Or "Would he call?" Then I would try to dig up anything that I could find about him on Google, Facebook, and potential background checks. I thought this was normal female behavior.

How I reviewed dates in the past was not growthful. I believed that I was stuck in the anxiety by myself and therefore I should handle it alone. It was my pain, therefore only I can fix it. Only I could possibly understand.

Then I "shoulded" all over myself, wishing I had done or said something different. Or I would start a pro and con list about the guy immediately, as if I was making a huge relationship decision after our first date. Rarely did I take it for what it was: a first date.

I never asked anyone for dating support. It didn't even cross my mind to share with someone I trusted their opinion of the details of my date. Maybe I was afraid to hear something I didn't want to, that it might interfere somehow with the illusion

> **"Rarely did I take it for what it was: a first date."**

that I was in control and could do it alone.

Perhaps more importantly, I didn't really ask myself "How do I feel when I am with him?" as if I was afraid to know the answer or that voice would somehow lie. Again, it returns to honesty and trust. I had to be honest with myself and trust my intuition and even my instincts which have and continue to develop over the course of my life. When doubt and self-criticism have become the norm, it can become very difficult to hear that voice, but if we're willing to grow, we'll be more able to rely on what our entire beings: body, mind and spirit, are telling us.

Coachable Moment: The Illusion of Control

One human characteristic is our seeming aversion to asking for help. We think we can and should do it ourselves. We appear to have more control than we really do, however. I mean, we have the freedom to grab the keys, get in the car, and go wherever we want. Perhaps we think we can get there a little quicker by speeding or taking a shortcut across the parking lot. But then when that plan fails, we get upset, frustrated, if not altogether angry at other drivers. It's their fault. If they'd only get out of the way! But what we should do is relax and let the GPS guide us. It's working hard so we don't have to stress. Use your trusted friends like a GPS in life and you'll get to where you want to go, likely faster and with less stress than you would if you were solely responsible for planning every detail, analyzing all the data and making every decision in the vain hope that it will turn out exactly how you envisioned it. So, sit back, relax, enjoy the ride.

"Where Do I Start?!"

Begin Where You Are

"Pain is the touchstone of all spiritual growth."
—Father Ed Dowling

Nonetheless, I knew I wanted to feel more confident with my body, mind and soul. I knew I wanted to be more in touch with other people and men. I was sick of trying to figure everything out alone. That was a starting point. After all, I had to begin somewhere, didn't I?

Little by little, I started to let a few people into the inner -workings of my life: a coach, a few friends, and some family. I was learning that fulfilling relationships were not found in the anxious zone, sitting all by myself with my thoughts and feelings, but by letting people see into me, the whole me — my loving *and* dark sides. I began asking a few close confidants their opinions and trusting they wanted the best for me. They actually gave me really good advice and respectable opinions!

The more I permitted people in my life the more I relaxed and the less afraid I was. I was more present with my thoughts and feelings. I shared my opinion more often. I focused less on trying to read others' minds and more on what I was feeling. This helped my dating career considerably. I felt like I had a team of people supporting me and looking out for me. I had a life team to call on pre and post date. This helped with my nervousness. I was more confident and willing to share my flaws. I found that the more real I was on a date, the more real the men sitting

"I was sick of trying to figure everything out alone. That was a starting point."

across from me were. It was not by the simple grace of god that my dating life was improving, it was because I was working to become a better me.

Coachable Moment: Intimacy ("Into-me-you-see")

How is someone other than me (i.e. outside of myself) better able to see the truth? Maybe because they don't have the veil that I view the world through. The problem with that veil is, it works both ways. Much like the proverbial ostrich with its head stuck in the sand, thinking "if I can't see you, you can't see me" the disappearing act we feel like is necessary as a survival tool just ends up hurting us. True intimacy — in any relationship, is the only way that growth can occur. If you don't let people see the real you, they can't help you. But, if you are transparent and authentic instead of being more concerned with managing your public image, your friends will be able to share their own experience and insight in a way that you can use and apply to your own. You may even discover that your friends know you better than you do. After all, they aren't nearly as concerned with how you look as you are. Ultimately, you'll find your friends more accepting of you than you are of yourself.

Most importantly, I have found that love is found in *all* relationships with other humans, not just dates. We can fall in love with humans in every moment and quite frankly our world needs it.

The bottom line is that Chris was the right man for me when and only when I was ready for him, otherwise it wouldn't have worked. I wouldn't have been able to see the qualities in me and in him that were compatible. If I hadn't been clear on what I was looking for, how would I have known what it looked like when I found it?

Ken's Story

"Listening is a magnetic and strange thing, a creative force. The friends who listen to us are the ones we move toward. When we are listened to, it creates us, makes us unfold and expand."
—Karl A. Menninger

I make it a point to always talk to my friends about my new relationships. However, in the past I never listened to my friends. Ever. You can imagine how that all worked out.

I have a very long history of making bad relationship choices. If she liked me, I was in. Regardless of how it seemed to my friends or how they thought it might work out, I constantly pushed my relationships deeper. When my second marriage ended, I asked my friend Luke to help me avoid long-term relationships for a while. I wanted to be single for at least a year. I thought my heart needed it. He agreed and he said he would help me.

Contrary to my commitment to singleness however, I then went out on as many dates as I could. Obviously, it didn't take long before I found a "keeper." She was everything I was looking for and I surmised that I would be a fool to let her go and try to date others.

When I told Luke about her, he was excited for me but he reminded me of my commitment to singleness. Yeah, yeah, I told him. Within a couple months, I was serious about her. At that point, I really had nothing else to say to him. I liked her and I wasn't going to lose her because of a silly commitment that I had made. Looking back, of course, I'm glad for the time

I spent with his girlfriend, but because I didn't listen to Luke, I ended up right back where I was before — with very little experience in being single. I could see, finally, that he was right to re-

> **"...in the past I never listened to my friends. Ever. You can imagine how that all worked out."**

mind me of my commitment, which I made to myself out of an honest feeling based on observing my own behavior patterns. But how quickly I tossed that aside for what I thought was best, or at least better, for myself. It sounded counterintuitive, but I had to learn who I was and how I operated not being in a serious, long-term relationship before I could be in one.

Luke is still a great friend. I'm finally starting to really listen to him. I've been sharing my experiences with him after each of my first dates and truly taking his words into consideration. I have to accept that he has my best interests at heart. This is what it means to be a friend. I don't think I'm alone when I say that I have had blinders on about my own actions while dating — especially early on. This is why we need our friends. We need them to remind us about what we are truly committed to — and when our actions don't flow from those commitments, that they care enough to call us out on it, even though we probably don't want them to.

Through the lens of a Relationship Coach
Molly Hillig Rodriguez, RN, BSN, MPH

What these two stories represent is that life is meant to be lived with a tribe, not in isolation. Creating a tribe is work, sometimes hard work — it requires intention and probably heartbreak because we are talking about humans here. Nobody gets it right 100% of the time. It's true that including others in our world is a risk, but Molly is saying it's really the only way to go.

Both Molly and Ken historically did not listen to their friends' advice. They may have asked for support but did not allow what they were hearing to soak in. Their focus was on immediate gratification, which, incidentally, they could have by doing it their way. And, despite their patterns, which were counterproductive to their happiness, they quickly returned to it. Changing behavior is hard, but we have to be willing to make the effort. Our friends can hold us accountable. Today, Molly and Ken are learning to talk through and trust experiences with friends and dates.

5 Actions Steps To Practice As Homework:

1. Reflect on the friendships in your life. Do you have close, connected and honest friendships? This will give you some insight into how you date. What did you learn?

2. Hire a coach to discuss and grow in relationships — *all* relationships in life. If we do not feel enriched in our relationships, we have no life to live.

3. Ask a few important people in your life to give you feedback about your dating.

4. Have a buddy system — call your buddy before and after the date and discuss how it went. Allow your friend to give you some feedback.

5. Look at how you currently review your dates and ask yourself "Is this working for me?"

Chapter 4

Meeting the Friends:
An Experience in Culture

Our friends are a mirror of who we are. Do you like your friends? Do you respect their behaviors? Meeting your partner's friends is an important event; it will give you personal insight and a view into your dates behaviors.

Molly's Story

"Never lose sight of the fact that the most important yardstick of your success will be how you treat other people - your family, friends, and coworkers, and even strangers you meet along the way."
—Barbara Bush

When I was living overseas in Bolivia, I learned some valuable and hard lessons about love. I had been dating Tiago for a few weeks, and my approach to dating was the same as in the U.S.; I was lonely, so I wanted to fill that void with a date.

Tiago had been late for our first few dates, but punctuality was not valued in Bolivia so I let it slide. I enjoyed the dates and moreover I enjoyed not being alone. Tiago was clearly interested in me — it felt like he hung on to my every word. He was affectionate and fun to be around. He was Brazilian. After going on the first few "hangout sessions," he asked if I would like to join him at a Brazilian party. This had to be a good sign. My other dates didn't usually turn into the "meeting the friends" type.

The party was quite the sight, with beautiful men and women everywhere, their long flowing locks of hair, tight and bright colorful clothes and killer bodies. Brazilian dance music was blasting in the background and everyone was bumping and grinding. People seemed to be having a genuinely grand time — laughing, hugging and seriously flirting with each other. I felt a little out of place in my jeans and ballet slip-ons.

Tiago introduced me to his friends and seriously flirted with them in front of me — I felt like the tarnished penny on the floor that no one saw. I wanted to hide. Then I realized all his friends were flirting with me as well — I got it! In this culture, it was ac-

> **"This had to be a good sign. My other dates didn't usually turn into the 'meeting the friends' type."**

ceptable to be gregarious and flirtatious. When we left the party in the wee hours in the morning I felt like I had received so much love from people. However, I did not know where I stood with Tiago, since we both did a lot of flirting with others. Usually, when you meet the friends, you get an idea if the relationship is going somewhere or not. I didn't know what to say or what to ask, so I remained quiet.

Weeks after the party I realized that Tiago never saw, called or texted the people from the party. It seemed like he had endless nights available for me. Where were his friends? I finally mustered up the courage to ask him. "Why don't you see your friends?" His response was, "They are not really my friends, more just acquaintances." He actually had something negative to say about almost everyone we met at the party. It was clear: I was dating a two-faced liar — he didn't have friends, just people he flirted with and then bashed. I was appalled, but I hid my feelings. I felt that meeting the friends was important, while he clearly did not, based on his low opinion of them.

My relationship with Tiago became more and more serious. I saw familiar red flags that arose from our night out at the Brazilian party. However, I was in a new country, surrounded by a new culture and speaking a new language. I felt like it was my job to fit in. I had made some cool girlfriends but we had not grown close enough to share how we felt about the people we were dating. When I look back, I did not talk to anyone about my relationship with Tiago — I thought I had to have it all figured out myself. I was an adult now and made the decision to move overseas for some big job. I felt to mortified to call home and share with my friends my hesitations about my relationship with Tiago. I felt stuck, but I put on my big girl pants and trudged forward.

Nine months down the road, Tiago and I were married.

"How Do I Know When...?"

Trusting Your Intuition

"When people show you who they are,
believe them." —Maya Angelou

After being married just a short while and still sitting with many hesitations, I found the inner courage to talk to my girlfriends. I needed to tell someone how I was feeling. It was like I opened a floodgate! They told me how much they did not like Tiago, how they thought he was a liar and they wished I had not married him. My girlfriends were telling me the things I did not have the guts to say to myself. I knew they were right and I was scared shitless. I did not want to be with a liar or someone who had a bad reputation and was clearly doing nothing to change it.

I ended it with Tiago, which was extremely hard. I was embarrassed of divorce and afraid to be alone. But I knew I needed a soul-scrubbing.

I worked hard to mend the holes in my soul after my first marriage. Today, I incorporate my friends into my relationships. Their perception and comments are valuable, and I believe they have my best interest in mind. Through my experience with Tiago, I learned to always listen to my gut and speak what is

> **"My girlfriends were telling me the things I did not have the guts to say to myself."**

passing through my heart and mind.

Ken's Story

> *"Be genuinely interested in everyone you meet and*
> *everyone you meet will be genuinely interested in you"*
> *—Rasheed Ogunlaru*

Date one was a success! We met online and went to a festival in the city. We laughed — we kissed, we took selfies. Date two was even better than the first. And date three...you get the idea.

I had to go out of town for a few days and on my way back she reached out to me and asked me to join her and her good friends for a drink.

I thought, "This is it, this is the moment when she gets someone else's perspective on me." The way I thought, it was both good news and bad news. The good news was that she thought enough of me to introduce me to her friends. The bad news was that I was surely going to get grilled by them and one wrong move or comment could mean the end of our budding romance.

My worries in the past had kept me scared and timid, so this time I just showed up as me. Or I at least did the best I could to do that. It was fun and the truth was, the things I liked about her — and the things she liked about me — were all found within friendships. We had drinks, we talked, we discovered things in common with each other.

Coachable Moment: Separate Friends, Separate Lives

Yes, it is important to have your our activities and special moments with your friends. However, some couples don't take this step in their relationship: bringing their friends together to grow their friendship circle. This is an all-too-common paradigm of having separate friends and separate lives, which is clearly not healthy for a relationship. You're more likely to become distant. It is so important, therefore, to take this opportunity to grow — to learn about your date — and maybe more importantly — to learn about you, by discovering how you interact with people who know your date longer and better than you do.

I also discovered that we all admired this woman I was getting to know. That became the focus — not me and my traits — we all focused on how cool she was and why we like hanging out with her. This helped instill in me a confidence that what I thought and felt about her was real and that I could trust that what was being said was true.

> **"My worries in the past had kept me scared and timid, so this time I just showed up as me."**

In my experience, the two things that make all the difference are being yourself and focusing on the amazingness of the one person you all have in common.

Through the lens of a Relationship Coach
Molly Hillig Rodriguez, RN, BSN, MPH

Molly is saying that everything that you need to know about a relationship is available long before you get married. She had access to the truth about Tiago, but just like in past relationships, she'd rather believe the fantasy of what the relationship could be than face the truth. Dating like grown-up means getting real about what is going on, who they really are, and who we really are. The time to get feedback is before you make a big mistake, not after. If Molly had trusted her gut instinct about Tiago and asked her friends for support, she could have avoided a lot of unpleasantness. When we are uncertain about something or feeling uncomfortable, that is the moment to ask for help. Moving forward she decided it was imperative to get feedback from her trusted, healthy friends and really listen to what they have to say.

Ken's story mentions the fear and anxiety that comes with meeting strangers, particularly when there seems to be so much riding on how they perceive him. Ultimately though he realizes that meeting the friends is a worthwhile, rewarding and absolutely necessary step in determining whether or not the person he is dating is who she appears to be. Not only that, but he again learns the lesson that the fears he expressed about being scrutinized before getting into the group situation were just a fantasy. Bottom line, when he can relax and know he has chosen wisely, it opens the door for growth in the relationship.

5 Action Steps To Practice As Homework:

1. Ask yourself if you trust your friends to give you honest feedback. This will let you know the type of relationships you build and perhaps where you need some work.

2. Review the latest feedback your friends have given you about dating or love. Journal your thoughts and feelings about it. Are they right more often than not? Can you trust what they say?

3. If you are dating someone, schedule a date that includes your friends. See how your date acts around them. Are they the same person or different? How so?

4. If something does not feel right it most likely is — so don't be afraid to talk about it with friends, coaches, even family.

5. Hire a coach you trust and who will challenge you.

Chapter 5

Meeting the Parents:
The Family Dynamic

The next step in the dating relationship is meeting the parents. This important moment can tell you a lot about your new relationship and family baggage. Who does he or she morph into when they're around mom and dad? Scarier still, you may suddenly realize why you chose them as your partner...

Ken's Story

"A lot of parents make you feel very awkward when you meet them."
—Stephen Chbosky, The Perks Of Being A Wallflower

I'm the kinda guy you bring home to mama was a thought I carried with me all my life. I'm not sure what gave me that idea or why it stuck, but perhaps it said something about how I perceived myself as a quality human being. I was very popular with other kids when I was a teenager and made a great impression on my girlfriends' moms. It was easy to see why: I was clean-cut, responsible, doting, and exactly the type of man most parents wanted for their daughter.

So, as I prepared to see my last girlfriend's parents, I wasn't nervous at all. We had been dating a few months and I was confident. I knew I just needed to be me and they would love me.

It didn't quite work out that way. We showed up at a family birthday party and no one came out to greet us. It was a struggle to even get introduced to the family as everyone was busy doing party-related things. Her father didn't give "the talk" that I usually received; you know, the one when a dad sizes you up by asking you what you are doing with your life these days. I seriously wondered if they weren't all just hoping I would disappear. I definitely didn't feel welcome and so my usual gregarious self stayed hidden.

After the party, I was confused, and talking to my girl-friend didn't help either. It was like she didn't even see their standoffish behavior as abnormal. Also, she thought I actually had handled myself poorly and it seemed she was embarrassed by how quiet I was and that I was not my normal engaging self. Ouch.

We were together for several years and even after doz-ens of visits with family and parents, they never warmed to me, and I later discovered that they simply didn't like me. Ouch again.

I assumed her parents' reactions would be different in

the future or just get better with time. The truth is, I needed to have a deeper conversation with her the day of our first family encounter, or better yet, *before we walked in the door.*

My girlfriend didn't want to talk about her deeper feelings and what was really going on with her parents. Their strategy was to avoid avoid avoid. It was hers as well. I wish I had seen it back then and asked for something different. If she was not willing or able to have the kind of conversation we needed to have, then I had to accept that it probably wasn't going to work out between us.

Coachable Moment: Princess and Prince Charming

Every parent's son or daughter is told at one point, whether expressly or through actions, that they are a prince or princess and that nothing, or no one, is good enough for their baby. With this complex, coupled with our own perhaps jaded view of life and dating, you can easily see how difficult we can be to please. Your date may have been told this same fairytale — by meeting the parents — it can make you feel like you've hit an impenetrable family system. Parents and family systems come in various dynamics (happy, angry, welcoming, passive-aggressive, etc.) and knowing this beforehand can allow you to be more understanding and less like a deer caught in the headlights. Having an *intentional conversation* about what you might encounter before you arrive on the scene can make all the difference.

"The single biggest problem in communication is the illusion that it has taken place." —George Bernard Shaw

Conversations like this are extremely difficult. That's why a lot of people simply avoid them with the hope that it will simply make it go away, like ignoring the 800 pound gorilla in the room.

I actually have some pretty real baggage. I've been divorced twice and I have two adult kids. This is a lot to take for parents that are still stuck with the image of a perfect mate for their child. Understanding your own baggage might actually help you have empathy for the way a parent is reacting.

Molly's Story

"...there is a difference between a normal mother/son relationship and a not so healthy mother/mama's boy relationship."
—Amber Benge

In my past, I have not had stellar relationships with my boyfriend's parents, their moms mostly. Dads liked me, but I usually rolled my eyes behind their moms' backs or just hid from them. *I just don't get along with women,* was my justification.

I also often attracted guys who had "mommy-itis," men who idealized their mothers and believed no one could ever be equal, never mind greater. It was clear to me that no one could live up to their mothers and I felt it, so out of hurt feelings I tore his mom down or complained about having to make a visit. The truth is, I was nervous to meet his mother. I wanted to be "his everything," but I felt like I was in second place — distant second place — compared his mother.

Coachable Moment: Two Kinds of Love

Nothing can replace the love a man has for his mom, at least in most cases, and there's no competing with that affection. But your love, the kind shared in a relationship, is not the same kind of love, or at least it shouldn't be. Therefore, it is critical that the man, or even the woman, do their "mom and dad work" — understanding that they are not their parents, or don't have to be, and that their relationship is different. Think of it as comparing apples to oranges; they're both fruit but there the comparison ends. Affection shouldn't be painted with such as broad stroke; use a more detailed and specific approach for your date and show them that you are not still "living at home" in your own mind.

This usually did not bring good energy into our relationship. When I started dating Derek, he was in love with his mother and I thought "Oh boy, another boy with mommy-itis." He told me stories of how great she was to him and his siblings. I liked that he thought family was important but I didn't like that he idealized his mother. After just a few dates he was excited to have me meet his mother. He saw us going somewhere, and I also wanted us to go somewhere. I obliged; this was different, I usually avoided parents at all costs. He said we were having dinner with his mother at a local restaurant.

"Anything you can suck at should make you nervous."
—Chris Rock

When we arrived, some of his siblings were there with their partners. Yikes. I felt cornered. I usually sweated and stumbled over my words when I felt super nervous. I was sweating buckets, and I just smiled to cover my fears. When we sat down, everyone was excited to meet me. There was a genuine warmth around the table. I waited for his mother's fangs to come out; they didn't. Soon I realized his mother was nervous too. She was a little reserved and stumbling over her words. It hit me: other people get nervous too. I felt a sense of relief.

I do not believe I would have noticed this without the work I had been doing with my coach. Historically, I would have been too caught up in my own drama to even notice how other people were feeling.

Derek was happy around his family and they were happy to welcome a new woman in his life. This felt new and certainly busted my myths about the families and mothers of my partners. Here's what I learned about a man's relationship with his mother: during the dating process, a man will put his family first. During a marriage, a man will put his wife first. He will move away from the home nest and family systems to create a new system with his wife. This is has been my challenge with men in the past: they were more interested in staying close to home.

> **"Historically, I would have been too caught up in my own drama to even notice how other people were feeling."**

Through this experience, I learned that I need to look at myself more and judge others less. Also, if I wanted to be loved and accepted by his family, I needed to love and accept *them.* Most men believe their mothers are the greatest thing since sliced bread. It is my job as his partner to start conversations around expectations of new family systems. This has been a process but it sure makes for better family functions.

Through the lens of a Relationship Coach
Molly Hillig Rodriguez, RN, BSN, MPH

Molly is saying that even the most ingrained patterns can be addressed. Just because something is a certain way, doesn't mean it will be or must be that way forever. Accept the inevitability of change and the possibility of growth. Humans have the potential to make remarkable adjustments to their attitudes and behaviors, when properly motivated (usually through pain). Relationships between our partners and their parents — and our own relationships with our own parents — should be open topics for discussion. Nothing is off limits in the world of dating like a grown up. Discover what your intentions and expectations are in meeting the parents. Decide that you will not get between them and your date. Just observe.

It is helpful to realize that everyone has baggage — baggage from their past relationships *and their families.* Be willing to look at it and share it with your partner. Don't be afraid. Nothing is as rewarding as honesty and trust. That is, after all, what a relationship is and what it should be built upon. And, it doesn't happen magically. You have to construct it.

Your date will be naturally attracted to what they know — what they learned growing up by modelling after their parents. If their parents were abusive or distant, that's what you're likely to get, at least when the chips are down and your date is back in the environment they know only too well. Don't be surprised or turned off by this. Molly's experience was apt — exactly what you would expect to see happen in hindsight. Despite Molly's fears based on her past experience, Derek's mom and siblings were warm and open to meeting her, and so she could feel confident that Derek was of the same mold. Derek's mom was accepting enough and it was Molly responsibility to climb over her past baggage.

Ken, unfortunately, had the opposite experience. While nothing could have been done to change his date's parents, an intentional conversation would have given him insight and let him know to take the lead in relationship building with her parents, or, in the very least, it would have prevented him from acting like a sourpuss. Few families like their daughter dating a sourpuss.

> **"...Relationships between our partners and their parents — and our own relationships with our own parents — should be open topics for discussion."**

If he was able to share what his fears and expectations were centering around the interactions with her family, the discomfort could have been lessened, and as a couple they could have grown their intimacy. Even if he simply had the courage to say "All my date's moms love me!" it could have potentially started a conversation, with his date warning him that it might not be so easy with her parents. Her parents didn't discuss things — so she didn't.

In dating, you have the opportunity to take the lead. What should be clear in both cases is that you get from your date what their parents gave them and you give your date what your parents gave you — unless you choose to break the cycle. The reward is two-fold: you get to keep your date, and

---

Coachable Moment: Baggage and Lightening the Load

Intentional conversations produce a unified front as well as a chance to learn about your partner and build compassion. Remember, you're also dating their parents, as well as ALL of their past baggage — relationships with other people. No human can just magically leave the past behind, especially if we don't even know it is there. Talking will help you both discover what baggage you are both carrying.

There are many kinds of love in this world. Some may even lump in a whole bunch of other, unhealthy behaviors with it. That's what baggage is. As an example, it may come with past abuse. While the parent or parents may have been, at times, very loving, they may have also been abusive, verbally or otherwise. Therefore, your partner will group abuse with love and won't be able to separate their good and honorable feelings from what's unhealthy. They will subconsciously seek what they know, even if it's wrong. Then they will mimic the same behavior modelled by their parents. The question is how to break the cycle. You talk. You identify. You work it out to create something different.

Action Steps to Practice As Homework:

1. Actually admit to each other that there are at least six people in the relationship: the two of you and both sets of parents. This will go a long way towards noticing each other in a non-judgmental way. (Hint — don't ever tell your significant other that they are just like their same-sex parent during a fight. Even if true — it won't go over well).

2. Plan together what your intentions are for situations where parents will be present.

3. Actually talk about your childhood stories (the good and the bad) with each other. Talk about how siblings interacted.

4. Get clear with each other on how you might change when in the presence of your parents. We sometimes revert to our childhood roles. Plan for this potential and ask for help from your partner in these areas if you are willing.

5. Hire a coach to help you get the most out of this very important part of the relationship.

Chapter 6

Are We Serious?
Breaking the Iceberg

For fear of hearing something you don't want to hear, you may put off asking the vital question: where is the relationship now and where is it headed? You may be the woman and be expecting him to speak up. Or you may be the man waiting for her to say something. Neither one of you budges. The solution? Share an uncomfortable truth to break the ice and reach a level of trust you didn't have before. Put away the gender roles. It's everyone's responsibility to communicate. Then you will learn what you value in a good relationship.

Ken's Story:

"Authenticity is a collection of choices that we have to make every day. It's about the choice to show up and be real. The choice to be honest. The choice to let our true selves be seen."
—Brene Brown

My emotions were running high. My last relationship had ended in flames but the new girl in my life was totally PERFECT. (OK, maybe I made her out to be perfect, at least for me). She had everything the last girl didn't have — starting with honesty. Oh, and she loved Lord of the Rings and the outdoors, which matched my interests. How did I get so lucky?

Have you ever felt like this? Did you think it was too good to be true or too perfect to never change? If you could only communicate what you were feeling inside. Oh no... I can see how this is going to end up. She'll think I'm crazy and run away, fast!

I was smitten, that was for sure. Yet it was only two months into our relationship so I wasn't going to ask her to marry me — that would be crazy — even for someone as spontaneous and romantic as me, someone who had learned to be the real Ken, no matter what others might think, living a life of no regrets. The only issue was my fear of losing her, or more accurately, not being able to "keep" her, so I was focused only on how to solidify the relationship. But, in my history, marriage was the only way to make that happen. It's easy to see that for someone with two ex-wives, I seemed to be a dead end, with no alternative. Repeating the same mistake a third time was simply not an option.

We had shared several "I love yous" in the bedroom up to that point, but the reality was that we hadn't formally discussed the status of our relationship. We had certainly touched on our relationship status but I think we both were just feeling the whole thing out. I was still entangled in some unavoidable pieces of my last relationship and I had made a commitment to myself to take this relationship slowly. Remember, I had made a promise to myself to not get serious for one year. That promise I made from my own self-discovery — the true intuitive voice that I had finally started listening to — seemed like just another roadblock. There was no way around it. Except straight through.

Coachable Moment: Turning Points

Turning points in our lives happen in relation to every conceivable human dilemma. Making decisions is hard. If it wasn't, we'd all be better at it, and ourselves, if not the world, would be in much less conflict. "Old habits die hard" is a all-too familiar phrase, but it's the truth. Most of us never ask for help when we are at the crossroads of making an important decision, so we just go ahead and make it. Then we repeat the same pattern again with another problem. Then another. Before long we are frustrated and back at the same place, but can't understand why. Our thinking can become so one-dimensional that it's impossible to even conceive of another way. It's easier to blame others for not treating us the right way or behaving like they should. Yet all along we have to power to make a different choice — and we discover this in the painful moment where there looks like there is no other option. But one suddenly one appears. The proverbial lightbulb goes off. We still may be afraid of the outcome, which we can't predict, but invariably we learn that mistakes are just part of gaining experience. There is always an alternative, and it's usually just a single choice away.

"When All Else Fails...Tell The Truth."

Taking The Direct Route

"If at first you don't succeed, fail, fail again." —Unknown

The answer was the only thing I hadn't tried: having an open and honest conversation, tackling the matter and my circumstances head-on. At this stage in my life, with two dramatically-failed relationships in my rearview mirror, I wanted to date like a grown up. I wanted that more than wanting to solidify the relationship. Above wanting instant gratification, I wanted to create real love, love that would endure the seeming pressures of time. If it was indeed real love, it would surely survive conflict, baggage and time. I wanted to stop making the same mistakes from my past and I knew that I was the only person who could stop the mistakes from repeating. It was my choice: do the same thing I always did or do something differently. I had to choose.

So, I started an open conversation. I knew if I wanted an authentic relationship I would have to just go for it. On a long car ride back from a ski trip, I broached the subject: *How are we? What do you think about our relationship? What do you think of me?* It was in this moment that I didn't really appreciate her commitment to honesty. We had just spent this great weekend together and the words coming out of her mouth weren't what I expected. She wasn't sure. She had reservations. She realized, of course, that she had said she loved me, but wasn't sure if that was true.

Coachable Moment: The Three Little Words

While there is no hard and fast rule, saying "I Love You" should mean something and where you say it says a lot about how much you may mean it. That's why saying it in the bedroom can have an impact. Sure, in the midst of ecstasy it's easier to say, but it's less likely to mean something, or at least what you want it to mean. The difference between sex and love is another topic for another day, or for another book, but perhaps it is, in the very least, wise to examine your motives behind it. Are you saying it because you feel it or because you want the other person to say it to you even more than you wanted to say it?

"He who learns must suffer." —Aeschylus

I was shocked and hurt. It was an all too familiar story for me — I gave of my heart and thought I was going to get the same in return. I actually did, but it didn't look or sound how I wanted it, and so my feelings were hurt, my defenses raised. Ouch. I dropped her off at her home thinking that this was it — our relationship was over. We agreed to talk in a few days but not until then. The next day I wrote a poem :

Here Again

You lit my fire, God
I was fine
FINE

Just me and my kids
Doing my best

Running and biking like a madman
Spending time with friends

The pain of my former wife's leaving
The heart wrench
The daily "Why me Gods"
Still a daily reminder

Then you did it
You woke up my romantic heart
You gave me her

She's a vision
I can't help but stare
I can't keep my hands off of her
We can talk for hours
About anything
About nothing

Then she said it
After a romantic holiday in the woods
"I don't think I love you."
Huh?

How can this be?
What can I do?
How does this keep happening to me?
Again, and again, and again?

I saw that I struggled with being loved and wanting to be
wanted. I sometimes wondered why I was so willing to put my-

self out there when time and time again I got hurt. But I had to realize I'm not the only one who does this, and to cut myself a little slack and stop feeling so unique and alone. That only makes the pain greater. Then I can usually come back to the idea that there is no other choice really — I can either have all of the experience of love or none of it. If I close my heart off, I will be safe, but then life without love sounds even worse than the pain that comes with it.

I did some soul-searching, sifting through my hurt feelings to get to the bottom of why I felt the way I did and how I could possibly change it. This allowed me to discover what my inner truth was as well as my outward reality. Therein lied a choice: to do something differently, to take a chance without any expectations attached, devoid of inward or outward pressure, cutting through my years of conditioning, and honoring what was right for me. I realized I had noth-

> **"...I sometimes wondered why I was so willing to put myself out there when time and time again I got hurt."**

ing to lose by taking a chance at being satisfied, versus the certitude of my familiar friend misery. So, I reached out again a few days later, and asked her out on a date. She said, "Yes."

On the way downtown, we had another brutally honest conversation. I went for it, laying my heart on the line by sharing what was on my mind without restraint. That made it possible to find common ground. Yes, we liked each other. Yes, we both had stuff we needed to work on. Yes, we could start over. Yes, we were both committed to authenticity and for now that was a great place to start. We ended up having one of the best dates of our relationship.

That can only work, however, if both people are involved and engaged in the conversation. I could only be responsible for my part; if she didn't want to play along, I would have no choice to accept it. Again, I had to let go of control and allow whatever was going to happen, happen. There was freedom in that.

My biggest lesson from living this story was that doing life authentically is hard...but worth it. In the long run, however, it isn't any harder than not living that way for years — or my whole life — it just took longer to catch up to me. And catch up to me it did. Being a grown up means taking responsibility for my own life — my own choices — my own lack of communication — and doing something about it.

I also learned that I'm OK. I'm OK when I tell the truth and I'll be OK if my relationship ends. I'd like to think that I'm choosing to be more and more truthful in my relationships, with the result being that there is more and more realness in my life.

Molly's story

"We are afraid to care too much, for fear that the other person does not care at all." —Eleanor Roosevelt

Are we serious? This was a question I usually avoided. I rarely even knew if I was serious or I just wanted the attention of a man. Therefore, a lot of my pseudo-relationships slid into just long-term hangout sessions, void of commitment and communication. By that time I usually felt too uncomfortable to have the "are we serious?" conversation, so the relationship just went on until one of us bailed. When Chris (my now husband) broached the subject, the story went a little differently.

Chris and I were about to run a duathlon, a run/bike race, on one of our early dates, when he said "So, I would like to call you my girlfriend, is that OK?" I was caught off guard; this was new territory. A question I was too scared to ask was being laid out on the table in front of me, and it was up to me to answer. I didn't know if it was a blessing or a curse. Yikes! How honest. How scary.

Chris and I had only been dating for about two months and I was still learning to navigate honesty and commitment in my own life (or with myself). I had some pretty serious dishonesty and distrust baggage from my past relationships, and so being honest with him posed a big challenge. He was charming, attractive, athletic and a little reserved around me — similar qualities to my

> **"I rarely even knew if I was serious or I just wanted the attention of a man."**

past boyfriends and I was a fearful to walk down the same path. However, one thing that was notably different about my relationship with Chris was that he was willing to share and ask for the things he wanted. I historically was afraid to ask because I feared to hear the answer. But his energy was powerful and captivating and I felt more comfortable around him.

I also felt more desired because of this, but the truth was, I was *allowing myself to be more desired.* I responded "Yes, you can call me your girlfriend." I had an instant feeling of relief! We were finally out of the "hangout zone" and into something worthy. I wasn't quite sure what it all meant but I wasn't afraid to ask anymore. In any case it alleviated a lot of doubt; even if it seemed like all-new territory for me I was relieved that it wasn't the same old stuck place that I was all-too familiar with. After our race, we had a new conversation...what does being serious mean to each of us? Followed by a big nap.

That was the first time in my dating career that I really valued myself. In a way, Chris had showed me how to value myself by asking me a straightforward question rather than just assuming or avoiding the subject altogether. I had stepped into uncomfortable conversations and stated what I wanted. It was new, comforting and a bit scary all at the same time. *This must be what dating like an adult is* I thought.

Through the Lens of a Relationship Coach
Molly Hillig Rodriguez, RN, BSN, MPH

Ken's story is instructive in that he was faced with a difficult decision and found the courage to make the right one *for himself.* He could either continue the same pattern of getting hurt and learning nothing, or give himself and his relationship a chance by changing the way he responded to hearing the bad news from his girlfriend. He felt that in the past he gave more love than he received and found himself about to reenact the same painful pattern, which would result in another failed, dissolved relationship. All he really knew in his heart was he wanted something different and realized that only he could create it.

Avoiding the truth because it's too painful to hear was the cause for his troubles, but accepting honesty from others, even though it hurts, allowed him to begin to grow up and out of it. He saw that honesty was a two-way street: he had to speak the truth as well as listen to it from others. When Ken decided to live the way he wanted to live, not just what he was more accustomed to, he found the necessary power to change his inner and outward life. As a result, the relationship continued.

Perhaps Ken's asking his date "How are we?" wasn't the ideal phrasing, putting most if not all of the pressure on his girlfriend. Instead he could have stuck to his own feelings solely, possibly saying: "This is how I am feeling and interpreting our relationship, now how about you?" It then becomes more about him and his feelings, which is the more authentic way to go, remembering that he is not responsible for the way she feels nor what she says. Then he can speak his heart and be prepared to listen to what she has on her mind.

Molly is saying something critical here, that it's the stuff that scares us we need to address. She encourages you to step out of your comfort/safe zone and see what shows up. She discovers that it's Chris' novel honesty and willingness to ask difficult questions (and listen for the answer) that contributes to a higher level of truth in their relationship, which is essential to its long-term health. Certainly, it wouldn't continue very long with a high level of doubt, as was evidenced by her past relationships that entered into and finally went past the "are we serious?" zone and ultimately just fizzled out.

Molly is also saying that you may also need support during these moments and that's OK. When you're so accustomed to avoidance and uncertainty, it can be difficult to learn new patterns that will contribute to longevity in a relationship. You won't learn it overnight, but if you're honest — even if you just say "I don't know" it's better than making up something, lying to yourself and your partner in the process. At the same time, you will learn a lot about your dating partner by how they respond to your honesty.

---

5 Action Steps to Practice as Homework:

1. Ask yourself about what conversations you have avoided in the past. What did avoiding them truly solve? How would being honest have improved these situations?

2. Inventory what you love about your relationship and what you want more of. This will help you discover what you value in the relationship. Share this with your partner and see what happens.

3. Consider your own future and think about the impact that NOT having real conversations could have on it.

4. Let someone go who is not willing to have "are we serious?" conversation.

5. Work with a good coach.

Chapter 7

The Bedroom:
Talking About It

Some people use sex as a way to express their feelings, and so perhaps they're guilty of confusing love with sex. Others use it to try to control other people, to get them to stay in the relationship when they'd otherwise leave, or try to gain power by withholding it. While there is no right or wrong per se, to avoid any sexual pitfalls, it's important to talk about what it is you are looking for in sex and to understand what your partner's perspective on it is. Feel free to discuss the topic of sex openly and move past any shame that you may equate with it (i.e. baggage). Shame has been defined as "covering up what is" so don't be afraid to uncover the truth about who you are in regards to sex.

Ken's Story

*"Everyone is thinking about it — why do we have such
a hard time talking about it?"*

So, my place or yours?

We had been on several dates. We'd seen each other 15 days in a row and somehow we had avoided the bedroom. As we stood there in the street, ready to go our separate ways, when I said to her, "I've loved getting to know you the last few weeks, and I'd love to spend the night with you tonight. Where would you like to go? My place or yours?"

She thought for a moment and I sensed she was working through some of her own sexual boundaries. "Your place," she said. We had an amazing night of sex, but it was much deeper, it was physical intimacy. That night set the tone for the rest of our sexual experiences together.

I feel that dating and sex are inseparable and so there comes a time when I have to address it. The only question is when is the right time? I have no problem talking about it, but my girlfriend might, so I have to do so with the utmost care and respect. Sitting on my date's couch after a wonderful evening is not the time for me to decide if I want to have sex for the first time with her. At that point I am lusting all over her and my body only wants one thing. My mind, perhaps understandably, disengages and allows my instinctual drives to take over. Some things don't need words but most things do. Usually by the third date I will bring up the topic to see how she feels about it.

I know how *I* feel about it. I am a man, I think about sex. I desire physical intimacy with a woman. However, with a lot of dating experience in my past by this point, I know that the

Coachable Moment: Having "The Talk"

It's reasonable, at a certain stage, to have "the talk." Society represents that women want to be clear about where the relationship is going before committing to "going all the way" with someone. However, the truth is it's a conversation that we have with ourselves that's of vital importance. Ask yourself if are you ready to give your body and heart to someone. Sex is and should be about people coming together to create a deeper relationship, not immediate gratification, power, manipulation or control.

It may be stereotypical to assume that the guy is *always willing and ready,* but in truth his body will let you know. If you end up sleeping together and you don't talk about it first, each of you could have different opinions about what it meant and once you've done it, there's no going back. Saying something like "Is there anyone else?" or "Are we exclusive?" can determine whether or not it's just casual sex or is a step in growing the relationship towards more intimacy.

relationship needs a solid foundation before moving into the bedroom.

One of my ex-girlfriends and I had an agreement once we started having sex. We weren't exclusive, but neither of us wanted to be one of several partners — so we agreed that if we started sleeping with someone else, we would tell the other person. I had another woman I dated who didn't ever want to be sexually exclusive in her life. It was a deal breaker for her and frankly — it was for me as well. Bottom line it's different for everyone. If you're clear about your own needs and expectations, misunderstandings will more than likely be avoided.

Molly's Story

"We need men and women to sit down and talk to each other about sex honestly and openly. But our lack of communication is hugely problematic." —Emma Thompson

It is clear to me today that before I met my now husband Chris, I didn't like sex. Historically, it usually felt like I was using a guy, but I would be the one who ended up getting hurt. I saw a lot of women in my life doing the same, so it did not seem unusual. Perhaps I just thought that it was part of dating for a female.

Women can be very vulnerable around sex, and I was no different, but I often desired more closeness with the men in my life. It seemed obvious that I could achieve this through sex, and they would naturally understand my unspoken feelings — that I was interested in them. Of course, I didn't discuss my desires but only showed them in a physical way. I believed the guy would just get it. But that was a huge misconception. Truthfully, men are as confused about sex as women. Only honesty, achieved through conversation, can let your partner know how you feel.

Today, I see that sex can be something beautiful: a creation of wholeness between two halves, but for this to be able to nurture both individuals, there has to be a good foundation first. Historically, I would jump in too quickly, feeling like I had it under control, but afterwards I felt empty and scared. If I really liked a guy I hoped that sleeping with him meant "sealing the deal." Very quickly I realized my hopes were wrong. If I left my goods out, someone would surely take them, and because I didn't talk about it, we were left with mis-understanding and pain. I didn't want to keep living the same unfulfilling cycle. I wanted more for myself.

Coachable Moment: Opposites Attract

You've probably heard this expression before: "opposites attract." It's true in science, when under-standing how materials form bonds and especially mag-nets, which repel one another. The truth about this in relationships has to do with what we're looking for in a partner, which ends up being the qualities we lack in ourselves. Apart, male and female are simply two halves of one whole, and a relationship brings those different characteristics together to form a lasting (and hopefully loving) bond. It's OK to accept that incompleteness about yourself and the way to protect yourself at the same time is to communicate honestly about what sex means to you.

When I met Chris, I had already worked on a firm foun-dation of myself. I understood and practiced the concept of "my body is a temple." I believed it and radiated it. Chris and I discussed waiting to get to know each other before moving in-to the bedroom. Despite wanting to wait, I knew I desired physical contact, so we spent a few nights in the same bed just cuddling. It felt cool to watch the tension grow and the attrac-tion build. It was exciting. Trust was also built in this pro-cess.

I shared with Chris how I wanted to wait and the reasons why. It felt so scary to say I have had sex before I wanted to in my past. He listened and was comforting. Chris shared his feelings too. We really wanted our relationship to work. I felt safe, cared for, and ready. When we finally did move to the bedroom, it was the best first sex I have ever had. And the more we talk, the better it gets!

Through the Lens of a Relationship Coach
Molly Hillig Rodriguez, RN, BSN, MPH

Rather than simply assume one thing or another regarding sex, Ken has the courage to discuss this difficult topic with his dates open and honestly, without fear that it will scare her off. Truthfully, men are less likely to initiate conversation, and the very words "We need to talk" are more likely to send the man running the other way. His desire for healthy, respectful boundaries, which are only achievable by open discussions, clearly define who he wants to be sexually and if his partner fits into that concept.

Molly is offering something that isn't often talked about in the world of dating today: the idea that maybe we can put sex second, realizing that she often put it first and expected real intimacy to follow. The truth is, we can experience each other from a place other than just sensuality. Honesty is the key to getting there. She is also saying that just the fact that she did something different will create different results. The definition of insanity is trying to do the same thing over and over, expecting a different result. That leaves a pretty obvious choice: mix it up a little. You may want to try something different and just see what happens.

In both stories, Molly and Ken come to realize that the bedroom conversation is important to have with ourselves and with our partners. When we are lusting, we are trying to fill a need inside of us through sex. Knowing what sex means to you and where your beliefs come from will support you to understanding the sexual reality that you create. We all portray an image of ourselves to the world and we get what we ask for, whether our choice is conscious or unconscious. Let your next sexual experience be conscious and meaningful. Respect yourself and the rest of the world will respect you.

5 Action Steps to Practice as Homework:

1. Reflect on your sexual past. How do you show up in the bedroom? Do you use people for sex? Do you feel you give yourself away too quickly? Do you withhold sex in relationships?

2. Take sex out of your dating life for a second, remembering your body is a temple. Does your partner show you the respect that your temple deserves, enough to let them inside?

3. Look at your friends. How do they value sexual relationships and themselves? It usually will give you insight into your sexual behavior and beliefs

4. Hire a coach to explore your values and behaviors. A good coach will challenge your current behaviors and support your commitment to live by higher values.

5. Ask yourself what it is you're looking for in sex. Do you equate sex with security? Sex with Love? Remember, we desire what we lack in ourselves, so what is it you see in your partner that you do not see in yourself?

Chapter 8

Can I Trust You?
Being Your Full Self

Trust is about being able to be yourself around another person, being allowed to be the full you while your partner is their full selves, good and bad. If it feels like a burden, then something's off. If we can't be ourselves, we can't have intimacy. We become less fearful of sharing our "full past" or baggage, not just the parts you want to look at or have other people see. It is our chance to live differently, to confront, perhaps, the people we are/can be without avoidance or pretending.

Molly's Story

"A relationship without trust is like having a phone with no service. You just end up playing games." —Unknown

We had been living together for about seven months and were creating a home. This was a new and joyful experience in my love life. I had never created a home with anyone before. In fact, most of my life I felt as if I did not have a home. My mother and I moved around a lot and when we moved in with my stepdad he made it clear I was a burden to his home. In my adult life, I had conveniently cohabited with guys but never build a home of love. All was well in the world of loving like a grown-up.

One night after dinner I noticed Chris was checking his ex-girlfriend's Facebook profile. Ouch, it stung. I noticed immense insecurity churn inside of me. "Why are you still looking at her profile?" "What does she have that you are still interested in?" "What the fuck?" I wanted blood for the pain and insecurity I was feeling. His response was "I don't know." The argument went on like this until midnight.

"I don't think I can trust you anymore Chris," I shot at him in spite. I could see the sting in his posture and face. He charged at the wall and punched a hole through it. It was a flash and then it was over, his hand was bloody and I stood there shocked. I never saw Chris respond like this before. The sweet, caring, and competent man that I wanted to spend the rest of my life with just showed me a whole new side — an explosive side — and I was scared.

"I Don't Know Who You Are Anymore..."

Accepting Their Whole Selves

"Trust is one of the biggest relationship makers and breakers, because with trust a relationship is able to grow, and without trust a relationship will crumble." —J. Johnson

We were in an all-too-common situation: that moment when you learn something about your partner that shocks you and makes you wonder if you really want to be with them. I did want a life with Chris but so many thoughts were racing in my head, "Am I safe?" "Will this happen again?" "When will he do this again?" "Does he have anger problems?" "Did I just lose the home I worked so hard to build?" I wanted to repair our breach, but

"I noticed immense insecurity churn inside of me...I wanted blood..."

wasn't quite sure how. The old me would have grabbed my bags and left "the bastard" without a single conversation. The new me was scared, but also knew Chris was a great guy. We were both confused, and we both wanted to talk.

I knew this was a deciding moment in our relationship. I called my Coach. In the coaching session, I explored my fears, hurts, and my personal responsibility in them. I learned that it is OK for men and women to express anger. In fact, it is healthy when done responsibly. I was reminded no matter what the result, I am OK. I felt ready to express myself fully to Chris.

We met and I fully expressed my fears and hurts, and that I still wanted to be together. I also shared my expectations about him expressing anger. He was really open to listen and learn more about me. I also listened intently while he shared about his feelings and thoughts. I learned that he did not feel needed in our relationship and sometimes he feels small around me. I heard he was afraid to end up like his father who unexpectedly exploded in emotion.

Coachable Moment: Who Trust is For

You have probably heard the expression "trust is earned" but simply going through life not trusting humans will ensure a life of solitude. It may be healthier to give others the benefit of the doubt so that you don't have to continuously look for trouble where there isn't any. You will get hurt in relationships, it is part of the journey, whether you give someone your trust or not. In a relationship, going slowly and building up a firm foundation of honesty and trust will allow you to have the skills needed to handle the inevitable situation where you really need it. It can become a pattern to "cut and run" after one difficult moment instead of staying around long enough to talk, learning about your partner and yourself. One action seeks to avoid pain, which only puts off dealing with it, while the other is an opportunity for growth. So, trust is ultimately for you and not for the other person.

Together we decided to move forward in our relationship. We committed to continue growing as individuals and a couple. Through this situation, I actually grew closer to Chris. I learned more about "us" and we created a plan for our future. This, our defining moment, led us to a deeper and more truthful relationship. We were loving like grown-ups.

We all get angry and express it differently.

Ken's Story

> *"Forget all the reasons why it won't work.*
> *And believe the one reason why it will." —Unknown*

I 'm generally very trusting. I also rarely get jealous and for the most part I want to believe in my partner.

On the other hand, I was far from an ideal partner for my first wife, so during my second marriage, we instituted an open-door policy. This meant that we shared all passwords and other information with each other if asked. For me, it created a level of trust that allowed me to never have to check up on her. This all worked amazingly until she told me she had been cheating on me for several months.

I remember in this moment I felt betrayed — our trust was broken. There were moments I wondered if I could ever trust again, but even in these moments I am glad I chose to trust her. I wanted to trust humans, I wanted a relationship based on trust, so I had to trust. There was no other way.

Fast-forward a couple years, during my next serious relationship, Jen and I didn't have an open-door policy, but we did both have a commitment to total honesty.

Listening to her describe a guy she was dancing with the night before made alarm bells go off in my head. She was assertive in her observation that there was nothing there, but I didn't believe it. She went into a store and left her phone. It kept buzzing and his name was on the home screen in text after text.

Total honesty was necessary for me to feel safe. I wanted to trust her, but I didn't want to be made a fool again. Obviously, it was a lot for Jen to carry the burden of my feelings from my previous relationship, but I also think it's important to recognize that we are all human. For some reason, it is so difficult to accept behaviors in others that we are guilty of ourselves. Being unrealistic and judgmental is poison to a relationship.

> **"Total honesty was necessary for me to feel safe."**

We had a conversation, and I was clear that I wasn't proud of the fact that I didn't automatically trust her, but I needed her to come clean. I needed to know if she had feelings for him and what was really going on. She eventually shared with me that yes, she thought he was attractive and charming and he was totally pursuing her. She also enjoyed the attention and didn't want to hurt his feelings and tell him that she didn't like him.

Because of our conversation, she reached out to him and told him flatly that she had a boyfriend. The texting stopped. This was new for me; in the past I might have drove to his house and broke his phone — or worse. Instead, Jen and I had a conversation about our fears and feelings and the situation was resolved.

∽ Through the Lens of a Relationship Coach
Molly Hillig Rodriguez, RN, BSN, MPH

Trust is developed through conversation by showing the other person your true self, all of you, including your past baggage and future fears. Your partner reciprocates. While you may be tempted to create a boundary centered around anger, for instance, what can be accomplished through conversation can never be achieved by drawing a line in the sand and not discussing it at all. If you put up a wall, you will miss out on a learning experience.

In Molly's story, she is sharing that life and people are real and that love is not possible without heartbreak because it involves taking a chance by being vulnerable. The moments where trust is broken don't have to be the end of a relationship; you have the power to choose to handle the situation differently by discussing it openly rather than running away. Couples must address these areas for growth when they happen if they want to have any hope of achieving different results. Your past patterns as a dater should be clear by this point, otherwise you may continue to make the same mistakes, dating unfulfilled, and carrying around hurt feelings into your future.

She used a coach before she had the crucial conversation with Chris, which was vital to her understanding that he was just a person with a past and that leaving wasn't the only option. Molly could then understand how Chris handles his anger. Trust truly means the ability to be authentic with another person without being afraid they will leave. Once each other's behaviors and beliefs are discussed openly and honestly, each person in the relationship can have the freedom to have a bad moment without it meaning the end.

Ken has had different experiences with regards to trust. He wants to believe in his partner so that he doesn't have to wonder if she is doing something behind his back. Of course, he must be open to the possibility that his trust can be broken. He has learned that he should walk into all situations with open eyes and also be aware of places where he has trust issues and be open to discussing them. It's OK for him to share with his partner how he has been hurt in the past and that he also must be open to hearing her tell him the truth about other people in her life.

By talking about our feelings, we get to discover what works and what doesn't, learning more and more about what is acceptable in a relationship, focusing on recognizing and working on our own projections and flaws.

5 Action Steps to Practice as Homework:

1. Notice what emotions you are most comfortable with including and especially the "negative" ones (Happiness, Frustration, Anger, Sadness, Disgust, Fear). Why are you more comfortable with these feelings?

2. Notice how you respond in heated moments. Do you retreat? Do you get quiet, argue or try to make the other person see your side? Are you passive-aggressive and take it out on them or someone else in a different way?

3. Hire a good coach to talk about these difficult situations because they are often reflections of your past baggage. It's also important to have a "safe place" to have certain conversations that are very difficult, with or without your partner, such as in a coach's office.

4. When you read novels or watch movies, ask yourself which of the personalities you most relate to. Is it the hero, damsel in distress or the villain? Why do you think you relate to them?

5. What are your "deal-breakers?" Do you have any?

Chapter 9

The Crucible of Growth: Change

Relationships are not meant to keep us standing still. They're not an oil painting. Resist hanging onto the "everything's sweet/honeymoon" phase — the magical thinking — because it's not grown up. Expectations will come into play. Every relationship will evolve into something else whether we want it to or not. After two years, you may not in be love anymore. You must decide to work together or split apart.

Ken's Story

> *"If a relationship is to evolve, it must go through a series of endings." —Lisa Moriyama*

I had just gotten back together with Jen after a 6-month break. We had intended on going our separate ways completely, but something pulled me back. I felt there was so much more for me to learn about myself and about relationships by staying with this amazing woman. So, with a trembling heart, I asked her to come back. I was so afraid of being rejected, but I took a chance anyway. I told her I thought we should live with each other, that we should get on a path to marriage and build a life together.

She expressed that she was afraid too. But once we started sharing our visions about what the future would look like, we both started liking the idea more and more. Yes. We would give it another shot. We would go "all-in."

That night she had a dream that she shared with me the next morning. It was an image of her as a little girl taking a piece of her full body-covered armor and handing it to me who was standing in front of her without any armor. That was such a clear picture of what was going on...I needed to learn how to protect my heart better and she needed to learn how to open her heart more.

Jen and I were together for two years before we took that 6-month break. We then got back together and spent another two years together before we finally broke up. Our story could fill an entire book, but at its core I think it was about growth — for both of us. We grew together, we grew individually, and we also grew apart. In the end, it was exactly what we both needed to be better in and more ready for our next relationship.

> **"I needed to learn how to protect my heart better and she needed to learn how to open her heart more."**

I believe all relationships are mostly about growth. We can't control other people, so all we can do is grow, learn, and decide what we want. If it works out, it works out. Of course, it *takes* work as well.

Coachable Moment: The House You Build

The ultimate goal of forming a strong relationship is to create an environment for both partners where continued growth is encouraged. When we humans stop growing, we die, and the same is true for relationships. Couples that come together in growth become a structure model for others to follow, by which we can all create a stronger, healthier world. This is how we, as a species, will continue to evolve in love and understanding: it starts with two people, coming together, creating a lasting bond. While we can't control the world or the people in it, we can lead by example. It starts with you.

Molly's Story

"By leaning into your discomfort, you develop greater flexibility and open avenues for behavioral choice." —Eric and Devi

My crucible of growth is about learning to lean into my partner.

In my past, it was heartache when a boyfriend and I moved from the "whimsically in love" time to the commitment zone. I would get scared and think we were falling out of love if we were not all over each other. Then I would pull away or act dramatic hoping we could return to the whimsical stage. I didn't realize that dating and loving like a grownup meant you had to learn more about yourself and the relationship. To expect the relationship to stay the same — forever — is magical thinking. Old thinking. I had to do something differently.

When I met Chris, we had a beautiful whimsical period. We went on fun dates, hikes, sent scandalous texts. We just could not get enough of each other. Even after a year of living together we were still in the whimsical phase. I believed we had beat the odds. "Our relationship was different," I would think to myself. I seriously thought we would be in the whimsical phase forever. But then came a reality check; our relationship changed when he showed no signs of asking for my hand in marriage. To me this was a familiar red flag.

For the first time in my life I saw myself clearly; I wanted our fun stage to last, but more truthfully I wanted security. This is how I knew I was growing. I desired a lasting relationship with an amazing man. And for too many years I had been hiding behind the whimsical stage, hoping it would always stay that way.

We were sitting on the beach in Mexico watching the sunset. I burst into tears, "I thought you were going to ask me to marry you." Chris's response was "Oh sorry honey, I am not." It felt like a dagger to the heart. In that moment, I felt so alone. My thought was "Why am I investing in this relationship if we are not going anywhere?"

I wanted to move from "whimsically-in-love" to "truly-committed" and I was letting my needs be known. I had no idea what that looked like, but I wanted to know Chris would be with me through it all. I wanted a home, fights, children, being 60 and sitting in a rocking chair on the porch. This was new for me, but did Chris want what I wanted too? It was time to find my inner courage and ask what his feelings were. First, I shared what I wanted in a future. Chris then shared that he was afraid of ending up like his parents. He wanted to be a great husband and felt he needed more time to give me what I wanted. I told him I was happy with who we were and even happier to know we would continue to grow together. We decided we did want marriage, but we were just a little unsure exactly when in our future it would come. Rather than put my foot down and decide that since he didn't want to marry me now then I should leave, I gave him the time he needed. That was also new for me.

A year and a half later, I married my best friend, and created an amazing life team. I was willing to lean into my feelings and aspirations and share them. My courage to lean in changed our relationship. The more I lean in, the more Chris leans in and the more we grow. Commitment for me is about growing together as a couple.

Through the Lens of a Relationship Coach
Molly Hillig Rodriguez, RN, BSN, MPH

The crucible of growth — is exactly the point. Relationships are about growth or they die. When we grow in our thoughts, feelings, and beliefs with our partners, we look back on life with appreciation. When we stay stuck in our thoughts, feelings, and beliefs, we look back on life with regret.

Ken took a chance. When in doubt, it's always best to explore the possibility that you might be right about staying with or getting back together with someone. Knowing yourself better, you are better able to make such decisions — even with the fear of being rejected — because life and love, in particular, is about putting yourself out there. As someone once said, you miss one-hundred percent of the shots you don't take. Another wise person said that experience is what you get when you don't get what you want. Even if you ultimately lose, you and your partner will have grown in the experience and be better for it, which can translate into you being ready to meet that one special person who is also ready for you — for who you've become in your new dating life. Either way it's a win-win.

Molly is talking about vulnerability. It took a lot of courage — leaning in — to share her concern about Chris not asking her to marry him, which was her measuring stick for whether or not the relationship was going anywhere. Being vulnerable is never easy, in fact it goes against all our primal instincts. But by talking about true her feelings, she actually created the life she wanted. She saw that all her fears and insecurities were just that and by talking about them they disappeared. Molly could finally see that she had a choice to do something different. It certainly didn't happen in the world of her mind — it happened in the conversations she had with her boyfriend "in the real world." That's sometimes a scary place, but she had the courage to open her mouth and continues to do so. Like building a muscle, being able to vocalize your desires, beliefs and feelings gets easier over time, until you're able to seemingly do it with little or no effort.

---

5 Action Steps to Practice as Homework:

1. Create a vision! Sit down and write a 1-year, 10-year and 25-year vision as an individual and as a couple. See how you align and where there's a disconnect.

2. Share with your partner the reasons you would be hesitant to spend your future with them.

3. Continue working with a coach! Vulnerability and trust take time to build and having a trained coach on your team will render more authentic results.

4. Start writing to yourself on a weekly basis. This means journaling about the things you want, what you do, what you think and what you want to be different.

5. Lean into your life and your partner. Continue to look for ways in which you avoid discussing and dealing with your issues.

Thank you for purchasing and reading this book. We hope you found it useful and informative.

As appreciation, and in the hope you will continue to utilize a coach as you grow, you are entitled to receive a complimentary coaching session with Molly.

Please contact her at info@mollyhillig.com to schedule.